I Can Make

TOYS

written and photographed by

Mary Wallace

Owl

Greey de Pencier Books

I Can Make Toys

Books from OWL are published by Greey de Pencier Books,
179 John Street, Suite 500, Toronto, Ontario M5T 3G5.

OWL and the OWL colophon are trademarks of the Young Naturalist Foundation.
Greey de Pencier is a licensed user of trademarks of the Young Naturalist Foundation.

This book was published with the generous support of the Canada Council,
the Ontario Arts Council and the Ontario Ministry of Culture.

Published simultaneously in the United States by Firefly Books (U.S.) Inc.,
P.O. Box 1338, Ellicott Station, Buffalo, NY 14205.

Canadian Cataloguing in Publication Data

Wallace, Mary, 1950–
I can make toys

ISBN 1-895688-23-X (bound)   ISBN 1-895688-17-5 (pbk)

1. Toy making – Juvenile literature. 2. Handicraft –
Juvenile literature. 3. Toys – Juvenile literature.
I. Title.

TT174.W35 1994   j745.592   C94-930289-9

Design & Art Direction: Julia Naimska
Cover photo, center: Ray Boudreau

Toys on the front cover, counterclockwise from upper left:
Eensy Weensy People, Dinosaur Puzzle, horse from Build-A-Toy Set, Toy Train,
Toy House, Bunny Buddy.

Other books by Mary Wallace
I Can Make Puppets
How to Make Great Stuff to Wear
How to Make Great Stuff for Your Room

Printed in Hong Kong

A   B   C   D   E   F

CONTENTS

LET'S MAKE TOYS

You can make all the toys in this book. It's easy. It's fun. These two pages show the things used to make toys in this book, but you can use other things if you like. You'll find most of what you'll need around the house — remember to get permission to use what you find.

- clear tape
- colored tape
- white glue
- stickers
- pencils
- straws
- aluminum foil
- thin foam
- ribbon
- hole punch

- construction paper
- paper tubes
- paintbrushes
- tempera paint
- styrofoam trays
- pompom
- clothespins
- string

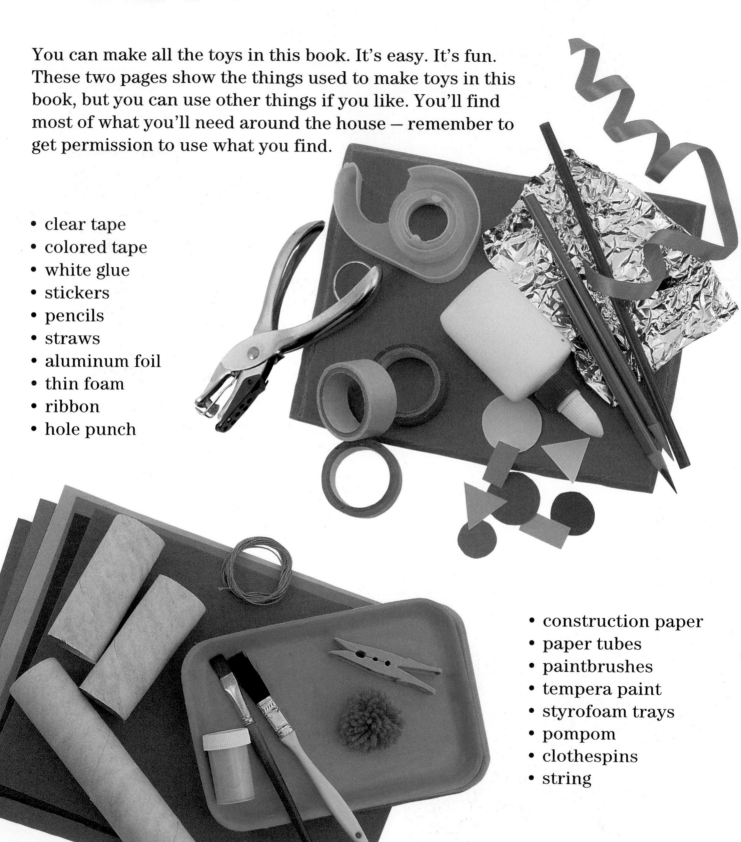

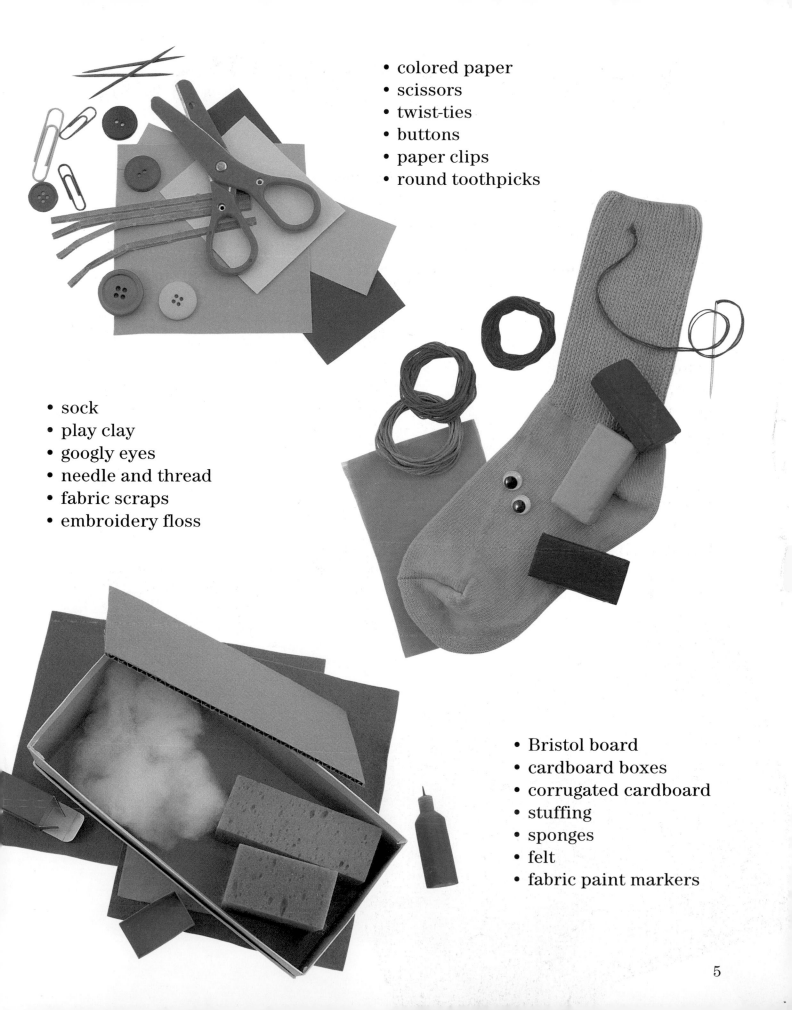

- colored paper
- scissors
- twist-ties
- buttons
- paper clips
- round toothpicks

- sock
- play clay
- googly eyes
- needle and thread
- fabric scraps
- embroidery floss

- Bristol board
- cardboard boxes
- corrugated cardboard
- stuffing
- sponges
- felt
- fabric paint markers

5

DECORATING TIPS

Hints for Kids and Parents

Use lots of color to make your toys bright. Before you begin, cover your table with newspaper or plastic to catch any drips.

TEMPERA PAINT is inexpensive and easy to use.
- use it on paper, cardboard and wood
  - wash it out with water
  - mix in a few drops of liquid soap to make the paint stick to a waxy surface
  - to keep it from rubbing off, make a finish with white glue (see below)

WHITE GLUE is safe and cleans up easily.
- use it to stick on colored paper and other decorations
- get the kind that dries clear
- let dry for 24 hours before playing
- make a mixture of ½ white glue and ½ water and brush over dried paint for a glossy, smear-proof finish

ACRYLIC PAINT or fabric paint comes in bright colors, and is waterproof once it dries.

- use it on almost any surface
- clean up with water while paint is still wet
- clean up fast — does NOT wash out of brushes, clothing or rugs when dry
- use a toothpick or fabric paint markers for small details

MARKERS AND CRAYONS are an inexpensive way to add color.

- use them to add details
- use mostly for small sections — might smudge if used to cover large pieces

COLORED TAPE AND STICKERS are easy to use, and they don't make any mess.

These are some of the ways the toys in this book have been decorated. And your toys can be even more special if you use ideas of your own. Be silly. Be daring. Be creative. Have fun!

FLYING FLAPPER

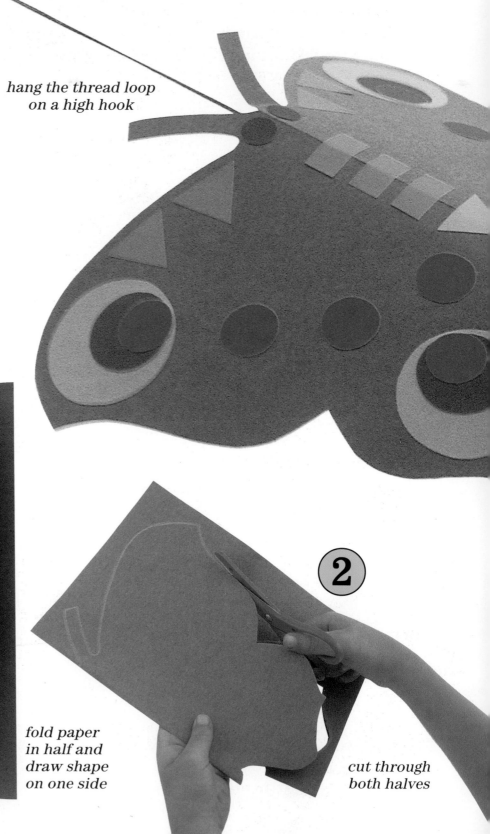

- construction paper
- pencil
- scissors
- stickers
- straw
- colored tape
- 4 to 6 m (about 13 to 20 feet) heavy thread
- *decorate as you like*

hang the thread loop on a high hook

①

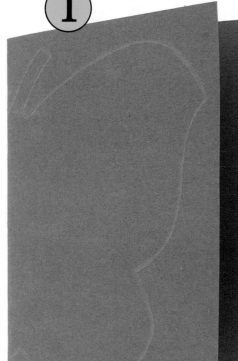

②

fold paper in half and draw shape on one side

cut through both halves

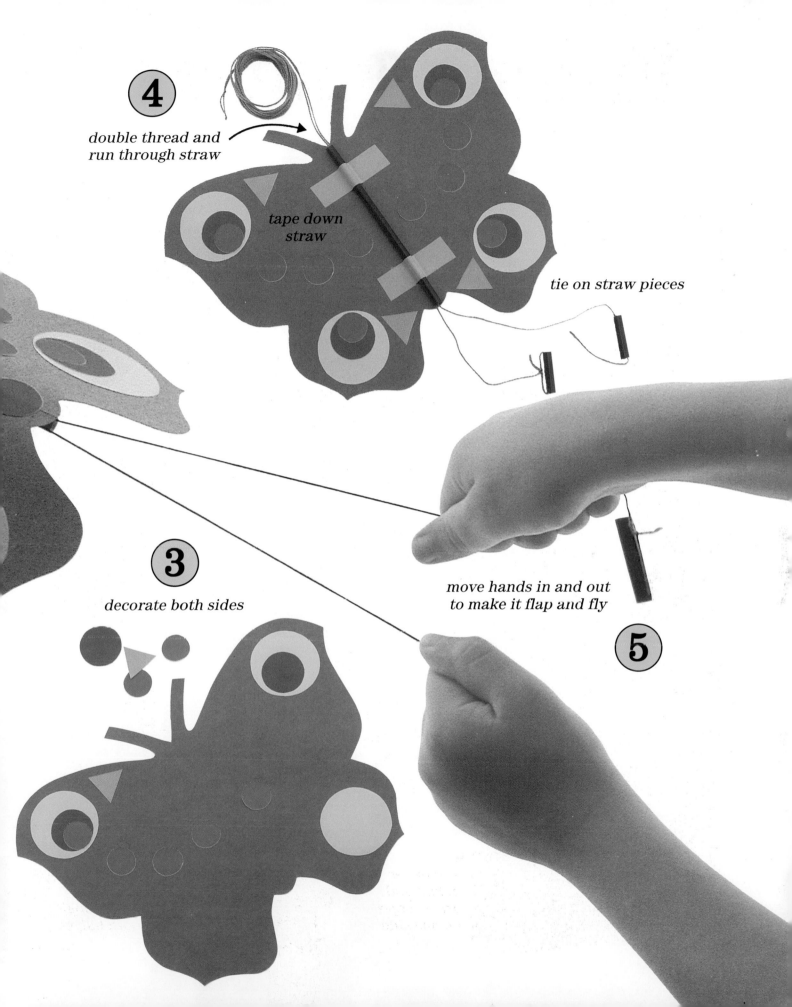

4

double thread and
run through straw

tape down
straw

tie on straw pieces

3

decorate both sides

move hands in and out
to make it flap and fly

5

TOY TRAIN

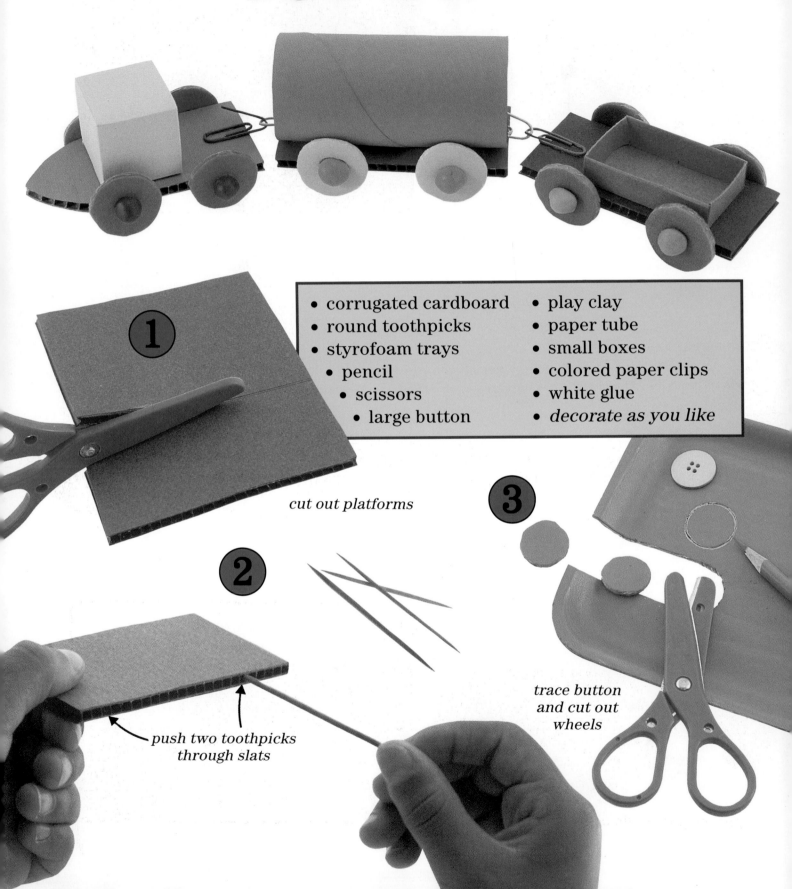

Materials:
- corrugated cardboard
- round toothpicks
- styrofoam trays
- pencil
- scissors
- large button
- play clay
- paper tube
- small boxes
- colored paper clips
- white glue
- *decorate as you like*

① cut out platforms

② push two toothpicks through slats

③ trace button and cut out wheels

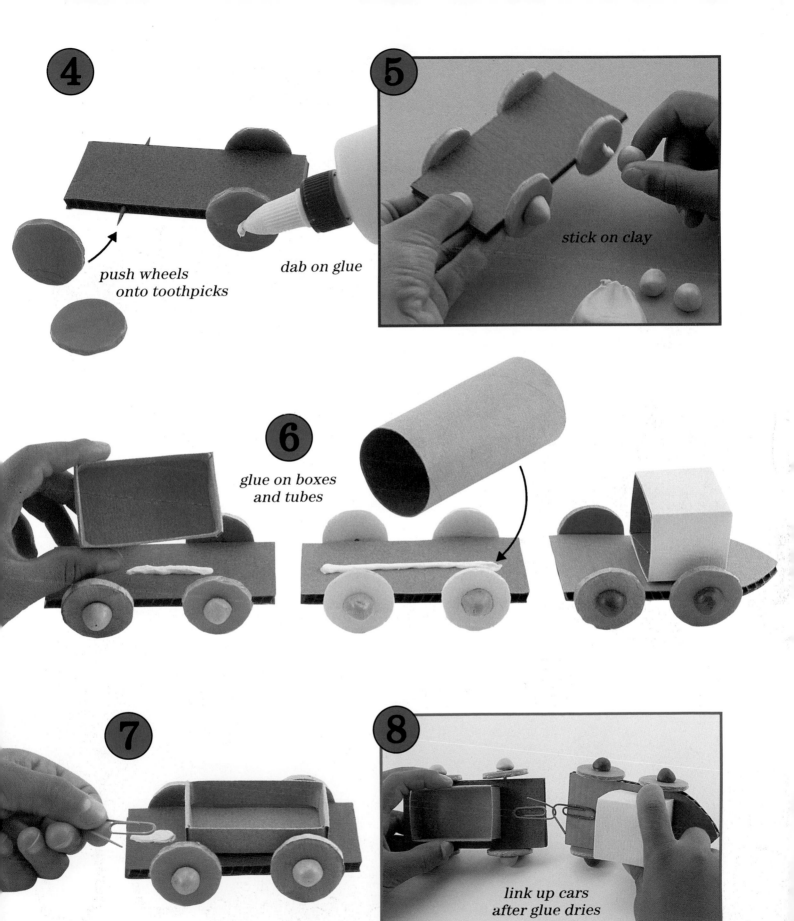

4 push wheels onto toothpicks

dab on glue

5 stick on clay

6 glue on boxes and tubes

7 glue on paper clip couplings

8 link up cars after glue dries

11

JET GLIDER

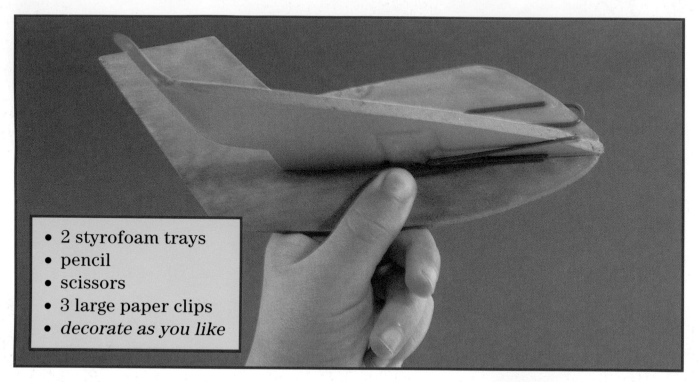

- 2 styrofoam trays
- pencil
- scissors
- 3 large paper clips
- *decorate as you like*

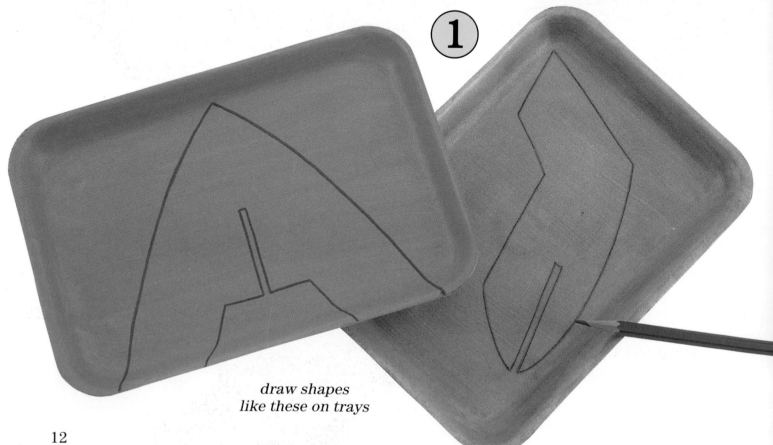

①

*draw shapes
like these on trays*

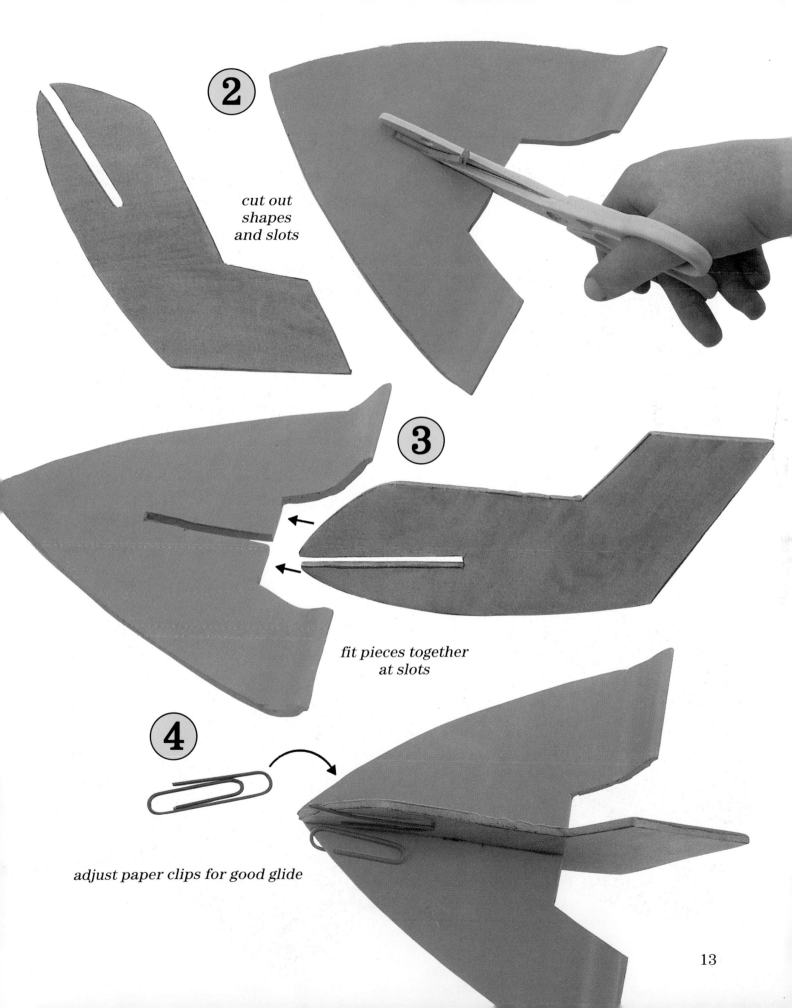

②

*cut out
shapes
and slots*

③

*fit pieces together
at slots*

④

adjust paper clips for good glide

13

RACE CAR

- clothespins (plastic or wood)
- buttons
- twist-ties
- straws
- scissors
- white glue
- colored tape
- *decorate as you like*

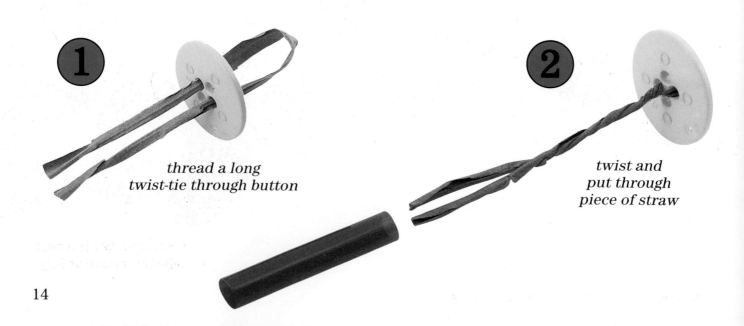

1 thread a long twist-tie through button

2 twist and put through piece of straw

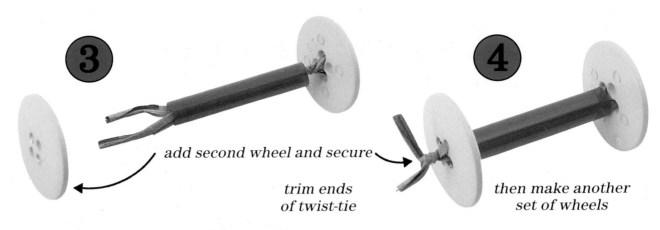

3

add second wheel and secure

trim ends
of twist-tie

4

then make another
set of wheels

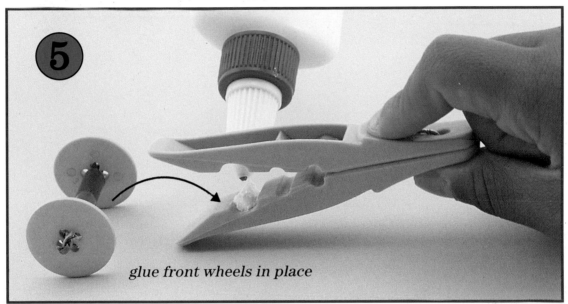

5

glue front wheels in place

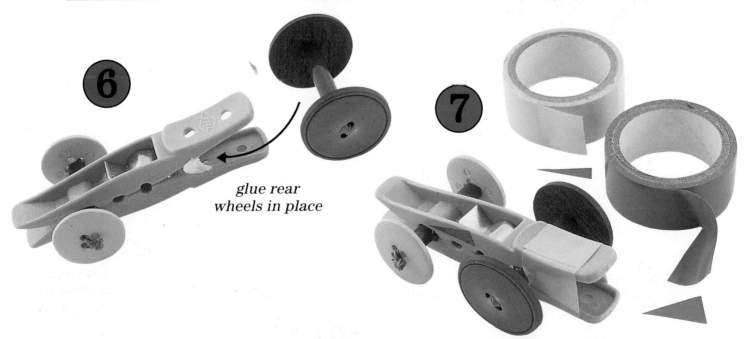

6

glue rear
wheels in place

7

wrap tape behind rear
wheels for durability

To make a race car ramp for your cars, see page 27.

BUNNY BUDDY

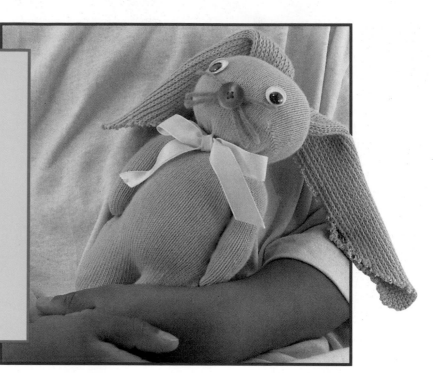

- *adult to help with sewing*
- sock
- stuffing
- scissors
- strong thread
- large needle
- yarn
- button
- googly eyes
- ribbon
- pompom

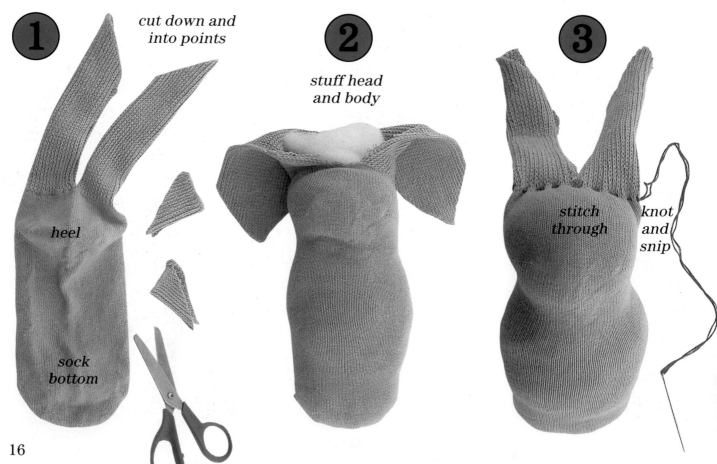

1 cut down and into points

heel

sock bottom

2 stuff head and body

3 stitch through — knot and snip

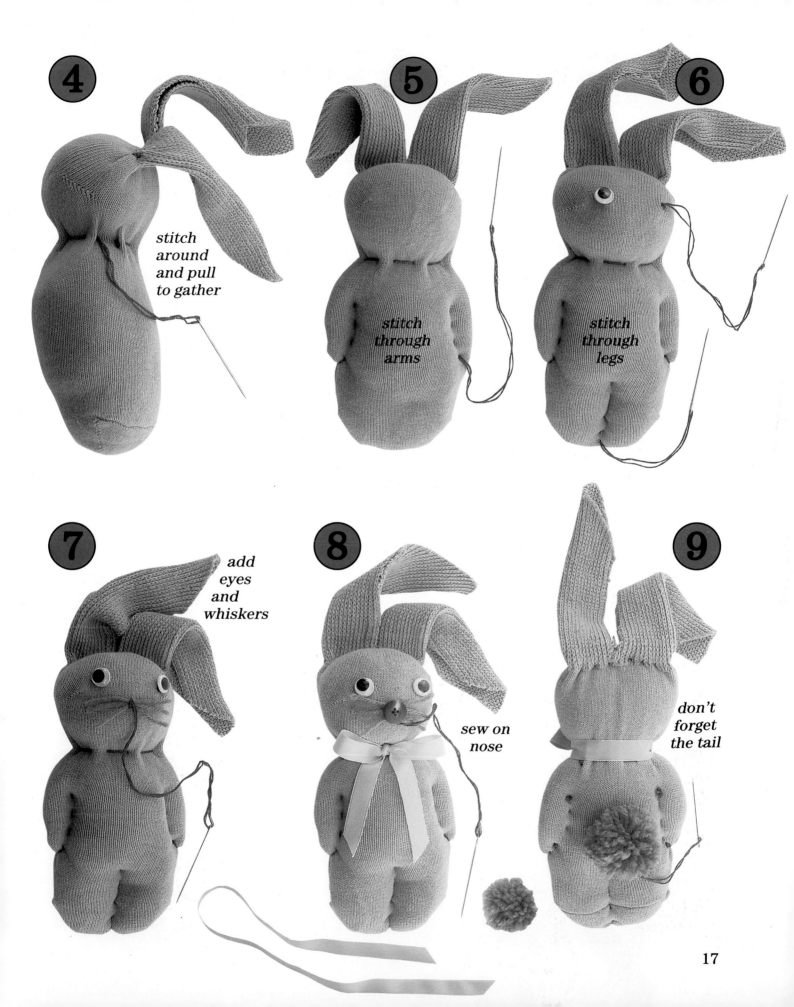

4 stitch around and pull to gather

5 stitch through arms

6 stitch through legs

7 add eyes and whiskers

8 sew on nose

9 don't forget the tail

17

EENSY WEENSY PEOPLE

- extra-long twist-ties
- embroidery floss
- scissors
- white glue
- acrylic paint
- *decorate as you like*

①

②

cut twist-
tie in half
for arms

bend another
twist-tie for body

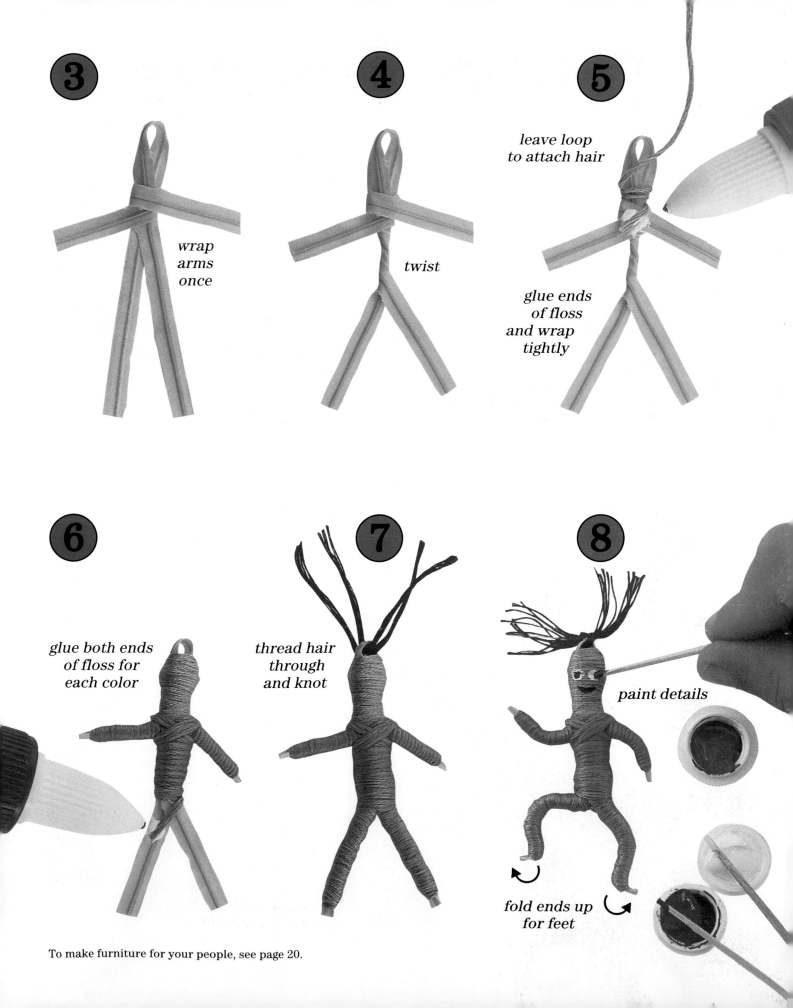

3 wrap arms once

4 twist

5 leave loop to attach hair

glue ends of floss and wrap tightly

6 glue both ends of floss for each color

7 thread hair through and knot

8 paint details

fold ends up for feet

To make furniture for your people, see page 20.

TOY FURNITURE

- sponges
- colored felt
- aluminum foil
- white glue
- scissors
- *decorate as you like*

CHAIR

①

②

BED

glue

glue

To make a house for your furniture, see page 22.

VANITY

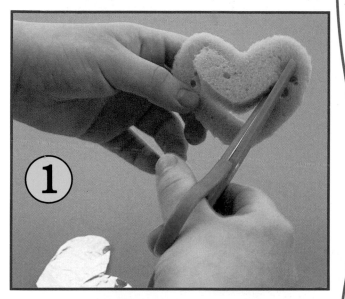

1

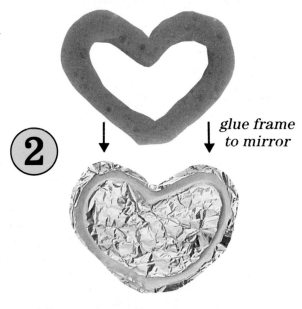

2

glue frame to mirror

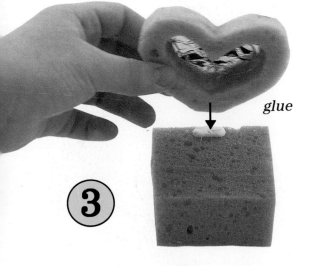

3

glue

CRADLE

1

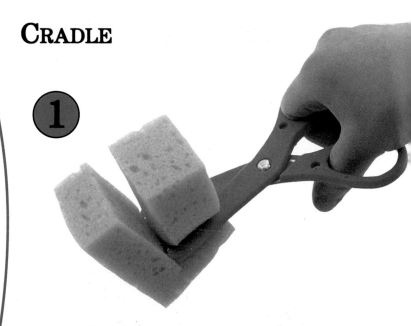

2

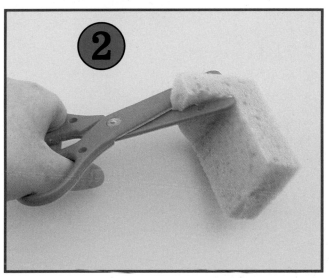

trim into rounded shape

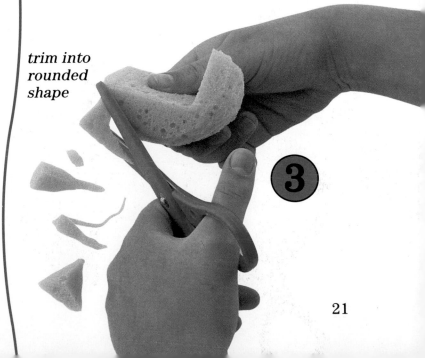

3

TOY HOUSE

- shoe box with lid
- pencil
- scissors
- Bristol board
- colored paper
- paints and brush
- straw
- fabric scraps
- small boxes
- clear tape
- white glue
- *decorate as you like*

①

poke holes to start cutting windows and door

fold back

cut off flap

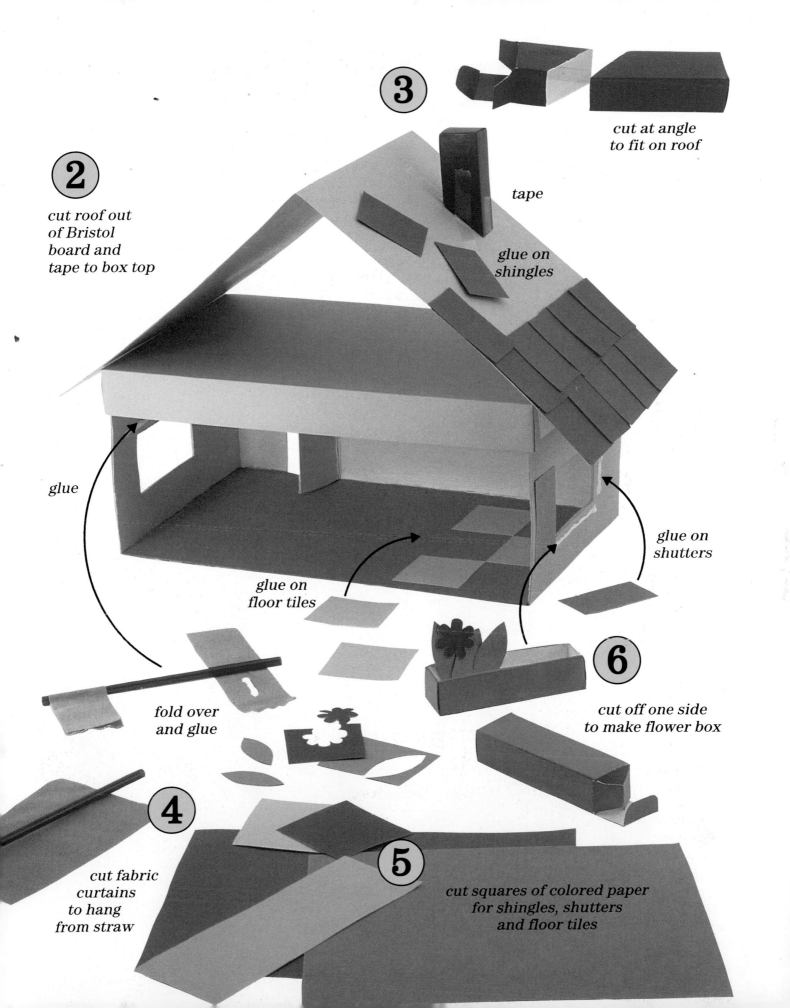

3

cut at angle
to fit on roof

2

cut roof out
of Bristol
board and
tape to box top

tape

glue on
shingles

glue

glue on
shutters

glue on
floor tiles

fold over
and glue

6

cut off one side
to make flower box

4

cut fabric
curtains
to hang
from straw

5

cut squares of colored paper
for shingles, shutters
and floor tiles

DINOSAUR PUZZLE

- tracing paper
- markers
- scissors
- thin foam
- Bristol board
- acrylic/fabric paint
- white glue

*trace
the frame
and shapes
from this pattern
or make your own*

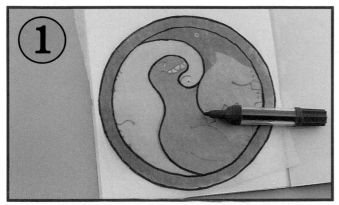

trace shapes and frame onto tracing paper

cut out paper shapes and frame

trace frame onto foam

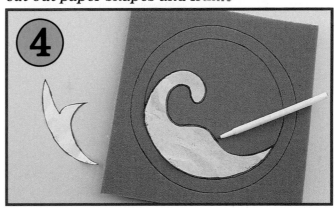

trace rest of shapes onto foam

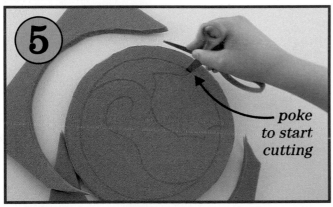

poke
to start
cutting

cut shapes out of foam

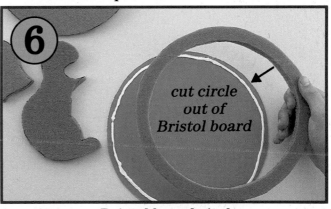

cut circle
out of
Bristol board

glue frame to Bristol board circle

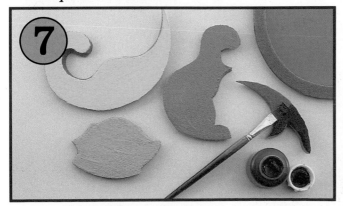

paint pieces and let dry

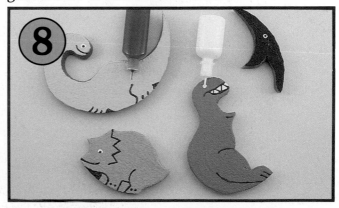

paint details

BUILD-A-TOY SET

- cardboard boxes
- colored construction paper
- paper towel tubes
- toilet paper tubes
- pencil
- scissors
- tempera paint
- white glue *(optional)*
- liquid soap *(optional)*

cut out circles, rectangles and triangles

decorate as you like

cut slits into opposite sides of each end of tube

Use white glue to keep paint from rubbing off; see page 6.
Use liquid soap to make paint stick to waxy surfaces; see page 6.

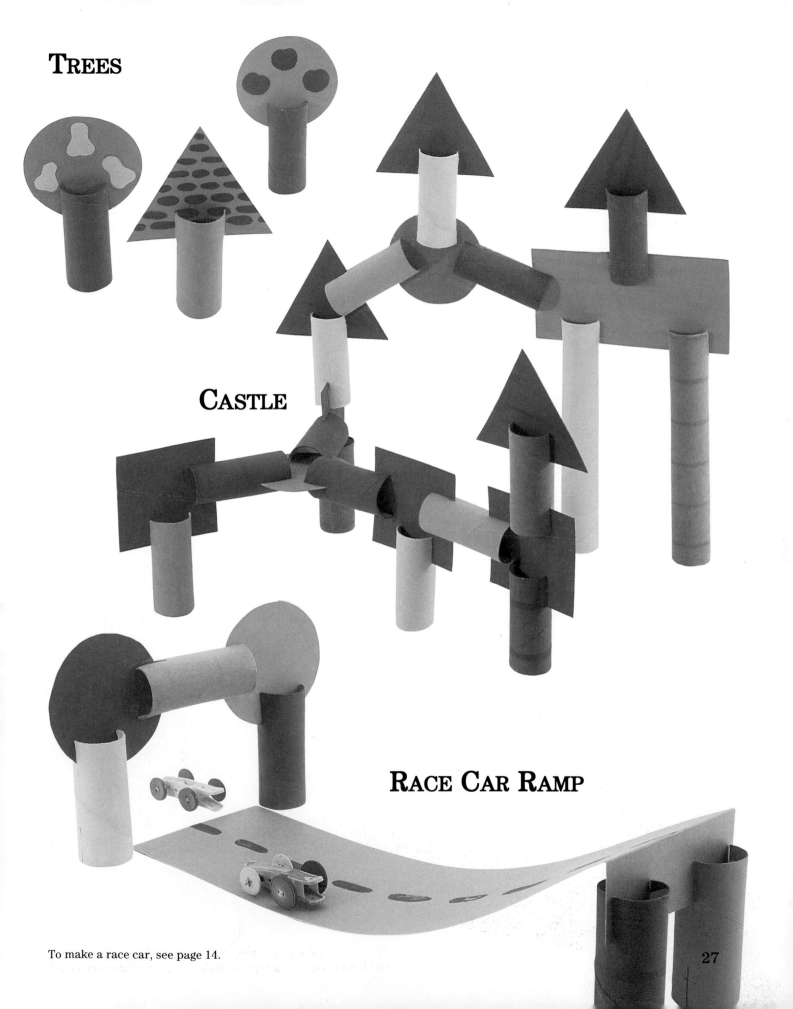

TREES

CASTLE

RACE CAR RAMP

To make a race car, see page 14.

Log Cabin

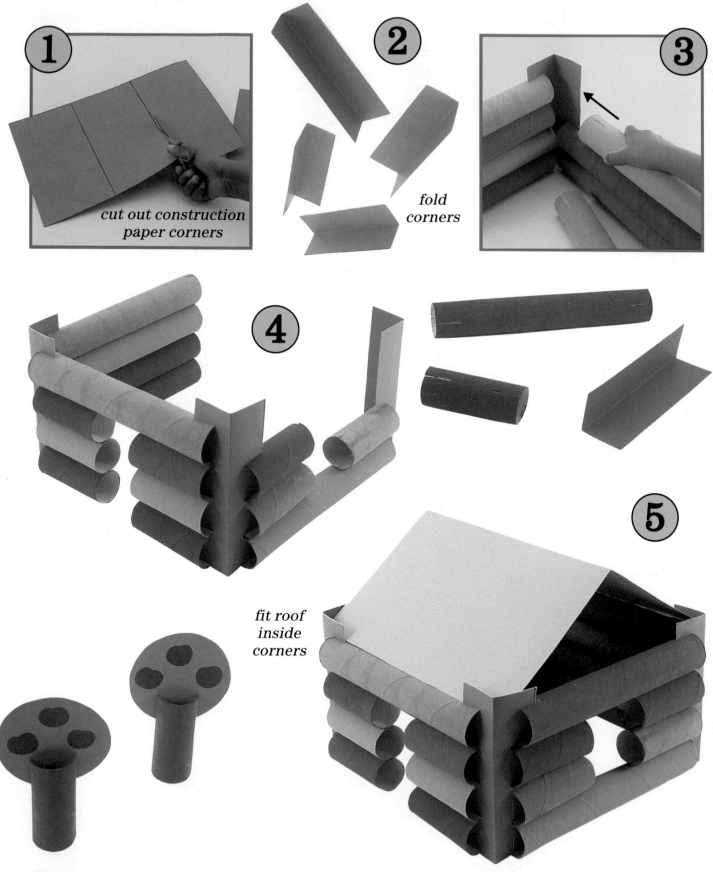

1 cut out construction paper corners

2 fold corners

3

4

5 fit roof inside corners

Horse

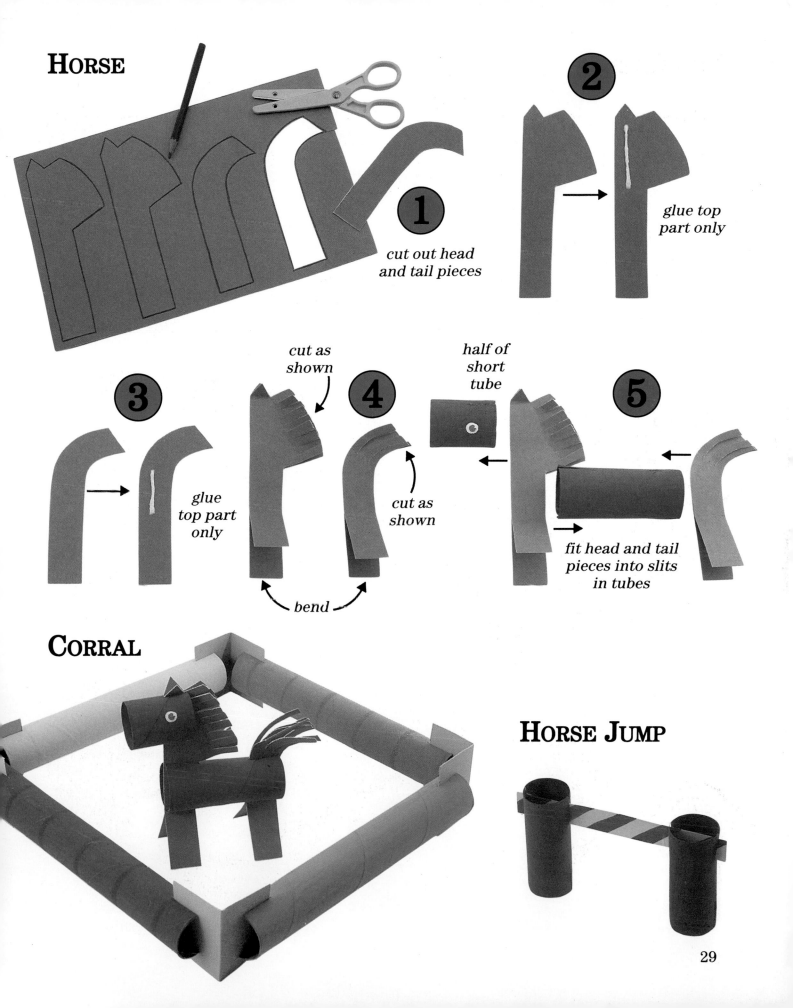

1 cut out head and tail pieces

2 glue top part only

3 glue top part only

cut as shown

4 cut as shown

bend

half of short tube

5 fit head and tail pieces into slits in tubes

Corral

Horse Jump

MY TOY BOX

- cardboard box with hinged lid
- colored paper
- white glue that dries clear
- water
- bowl
- pencil
- hole punch
- string
- large button

tear strips and pieces of colored paper

dip paper pieces into mixture and smooth onto box

½ white glue and ½ water

cover box and let dry overnight

*punch holes on top
and front of box near edge*

tie string to make loop on top of box lid

thread button on another piece of string

attach button to outside of box front

tie down button

To see the finished toy box, turn the page!